Kangaroos

Published by Wildlife Education, Ltd.
9820 Willow Creek Road, Suite 300, San Diego, California 92131

ISBN 0-937934-80-1

Kangaroos

Series Created by
John Bonnett Wexo

Written by
Beth Wagner Brust

Zoological Consultant
Charles R. Schroeder, D.V.M.
Director Emeritus
San Diego Zoo and San Diego Wild Animal Park

Scientific Consultants
Michael Archer, Ph.D.
Professor of Biological Science
University of New South Wales, Australia

Karl Kranz, M.A.
General Curator
Philadelphia Zoological Gardens

Art Credits

Paintings: Darrel Millsap

Additional Art: Page Ten: Lower Left, Elizabeth McClelland; **Bottom,** Walter Stuart; **Lower Middle,** Charles Byron; **Lower Right,** Walter Stuart

Page Eleven: Upper Right, Elizabeth McClelland

Page Thirteen: Top Center, Biruta Akerbergs Hansen; **Upper Right,** Walter Stuart

Page Eighteen: Middle Left, Biruta Akerbergs Hansen; **Lower Left,** Elizabeth McClelland

Page Nineteen: Top Center, Charles Byron; **Upper Right,** Charles Byron

Page Twenty: Top, Douglas Schneider

Pages Twenty and Twenty-one: Bottom, Biruta Akerbergs Hansen

Page Twenty-one: Upper Right, Walter Stuart; **Lower Right,** Biruta Akerbergs Hansen

Activities Art: Elizabeth Morales-Denney.

Photographic Credits

Front Cover: C. Andrew Henley *(Auscape International)*

Pages Six and Seven: John Cancalosi *(Bruce Coleman, Ltd.)*

Page Eight: Upper Right, Bill Bachman *(Photo Researchers, Inc.);* **Lower Left,** Jean-Paul Ferrero *(Ardea London)*

Page Nine: Fritz Prenzel *(Bruce Coleman, Ltd.)*

Pages Ten and Eleven: Top, Cristina Smith *(Wildlife Education, Ltd.)*

Page Eleven: Top, Phil A. Dotson *(Photo Researchers, Inc.);* **Right,** Veronica Tagland *(Wildlife Education, Ltd.)*

Page Twelve: Middle Left, Tom Stack and Associates; **Bottom Left,** Cristina Smith *(Wildlife Education, Ltd.)*

Pages Fourteen and Fifteen: Gerry Ellis *(Ellis Wildlife Collection)*

Page Sixteen: Tom McHugh *(Photo Researchers, Inc.)*

Page Seventeen: Top, Francisco Erize *(Bruce Coleman, Ltd.);* **Lower Right,** Chip Isenhart *(Tom Stack and Associates)*

Page Nineteen: Penny Tweedie *(Woodfin Camp and Associates)*

Page Twenty-one: John Shaw *(Bruce Coleman, Inc.)*

Page Twenty-two: Upper Left, C. Andrew Henley *(Auscape International);* **Lower Right,** Belinda Wright *(DRK Photo)*

Page Twenty-three: Middle Left, Belinda Wright *(DRK Photo);* **Lower Left,** Belinda Wright *(DRK Photo);* **Lower Right,** Cristina Smith *(Wildlife Education, Ltd.)*

Our Thanks To: James M. Dolan, Jr., Ph.D. *(Zoological Society of San Diego);* Terry J. Mulroney *(Zoological Society of San Diego);* Carmi Penny *(Zoological Society of San Diego);* Linda Coates, Valerie Hare, and Wendy Perkins *(San Diego Zoo Library);* Michael Hutchins, Ph.D. *(New York Zoological Park);* Margaret Rau; Paul Brust; Sean Brust; Kathy Landvogt; Peter Condliffe; Erin Stuart; Pam Stuart; Joe Selig.

Cover Photo: Eastern gray kangaroo

Contents

Kangaroos are fascinating animals. And some of them are the largest hopping animals in the world! Kangaroos originated in Australia, and today are the country's national symbol. They are also found in New Guinea, and on adjacent islands.

As you will see, kangaroos come in many sizes and varieties. Of the approximately 60 types of kangaroos, by far the best known are the red and gray kangaroos (a family of gray kangaroos is shown at right). These are the ones usually seen in zoos and animal parks.

Kangaroos are hard to describe. They graze like deer, hop like rabbits, and go without water like camels. But they are not related to any of these animals. Like koalas and opossums, kangaroos belong to a unique group of mammals called *marsupials* (mar-SOUP-ee-uls). And like all marsupials, they carry their young in special body pockets called pouches. The bigger kangaroos are the largest marsupials in the world!

Kangaroos and their cousins, the wallaroos and the wallabies, are *herbivores* (URB-uh-voars). They eat mostly grass, along with a few plants and shrubs. Kangaroos get most of their water from the plants they eat, which is good since water is very scarce in parts of Australia. Some can go for weeks, *even months*, without water!

Heat, drought, and hunger are the biggest natural threats to kangaroos. Their harsh surroundings reduce their chances of survival. The average kangaroo lives only 7 years in the wild, but some of the larger kangaroos live to be 20 years old.

What helps many types of kangaroos live longer is that they form groups, or "mobs." Members of a mob look out for danger and warn each other by sounding an alarm. The mob's leader is called the "Old Man." In general, male kangaroos are "boomers," females are "does," and youngsters are "joeys."

More study of kangaroos in the wild is needed to better understand these unusual animals. There is concern about the future of kangaroos. A way must be found to protect them from habitat destruction, while still making land available for farming and ranching.

Can you find the joey in the kangaroo family at right?

Western gray kangaroos

The earliest ancestors of kangaroos lived in trees. When they came down to live on the ground, they started hopping so that they could get around faster. Some kangaroos returned to the trees, but the rest stayed on the ground and are found today in all sorts of habitats.

Kangaroos are divided into two groups. The larger ones are called *macropodids* (MAK-roh-PAH-didz), which means "large foot." All the others are called *potoroids* (POT-uh-roidz). In general, kangaroos are grouped according to size. The largest are called kangaroos. Slightly smaller are wallaroos, or euros (YOUR-ose). Next smallest are wallabies. Smaller still are pademelons (PAD-ee-MEL-uns). And smallest of all are rat kangaroos.

Gray kangaroos and antilopine wallaroos live in open woodlands (pictured above). Male eastern grays are the stockiest and heaviest of all the kangaroos, rivaling the red kangaroo for overall size. Male eastern grays average 200 pounds (90 kilograms) and are sometimes up to 7 feet tall (2.1 meters).

LUMHOLTZ'S TREE KANGAROO
Dendrolagus lumholtzi

Rain forests shelter eight different types of tree kangaroos. Tree kangaroos live their entire lives above the ground — and only come down for water.

MUSKY RAT KANGAROO
Hypsiprymnodon moschatus

QUOKKA
Setonix brachyurus

ANTILOPINE WALLAROO
Macropus antilopinus

EASTERN GRAY KANGAROO
Macropus giganteus

BRUSH-TAILED ROCK WALLABY
Petrogale penicillata

YELLOW-FOOTED ROCK WALLABY
Petrogale xanthopus

The climbing skills of rock wallabies are truly remarkable! They can bounce up even the steepest rock face. You can tell where they live, because the stones around their caves are *polished smooth* from thousands of years of wallaby traffic.

WHITE-STRIPED DORCOPSIS
Dorcopsis hageni

RED-NECKED PADEMELON
Thylogale thetis

Wallabies and pademelons once roamed the grasslands of mainland Australia. But today they are found only on islands offshore, where there are fewer predators and no farmers to disturb them.

BRIDLED NAILTAIL WALLABY
Onychogalea fraenata

BANDED-HARE WALLABY
Lagostrophus fasciatus

9

A kangaroo's tail is *extremely* muscular. And it is long—almost as long as the rest of the kangaroo's body! Its most important use is for balance while hopping.

SEE FOR YOURSELF

Here's a simple way to see for yourself how a kangaroo uses its tail. First, put your legs together and hop very fast down a hallway. It's pretty hard to stay upright and not lean forward, isn't it? Now, stand on one leg and hold your other leg out behind you. Hop as fast as you can. See how much easier it is to hop and keep your balance with a "tail" behind you!

Kangaroos leap at top speeds to escape danger. But only their powerful hindlegs touch the ground as they bound from place to place. To move faster, they keep their front legs out of the way by holding them close to their chests. And to keep their balance, they curve their long tails slightly upward behind them. When traveling fast, a kangaroo is in the air about 70 percent of the time!

Some kangaroos can reach speeds of 43 miles (70 kilometers) per hour, but they tire quickly. However, at a slower speed of about 12 miles (20 kilometers) per hour, they can keep hopping for hours.

Most kangaroos have four toes on their hindfeet. The two inside toes are joined, making a very handy grooming tool. Kangaroos use this "comb" to smooth their fur and to scratch behind their ears. The extra-long middle toe has a sharp nail, which is used as a weapon during fights.

Kangaroos can hop for a very long time without getting tired. They can do this because they can store energy in special tendons in their hindlegs. Like the springs in a pogo stick, these tendons release more and more energy as the kangaroo hops along. The faster it hops, the less energy it takes for the kangaroo to keep going.

Kangaroos don't always hop fast. When moving slowly, a kangaroo shuffles on all four legs, using its tail as a sort of "chair." First, it balances on its front legs and tail, and swings its hindlegs forward. Then, while squatting on its hindlegs, it moves its front legs and tail forward.

Because much of Australia is hot and dry, kangaroos must be able to survive in extreme heat. To keep from losing body fluids, they seldom sweat. And to cool off, they "pant" like dogs. When it's very hot, they lick their front legs and chests. The evaporating saliva helps to cool their bodies.

Kangaroos use the five claws on their front feet as a "comb"— the same way that you use a comb. They run their claws through their fur to comb out dirt and smooth any tangles. Kangaroos spend long periods grooming themselves.

All kangaroos have large ears that can be turned in all directions. With their excellent hearing, they can pick up sounds from far away.

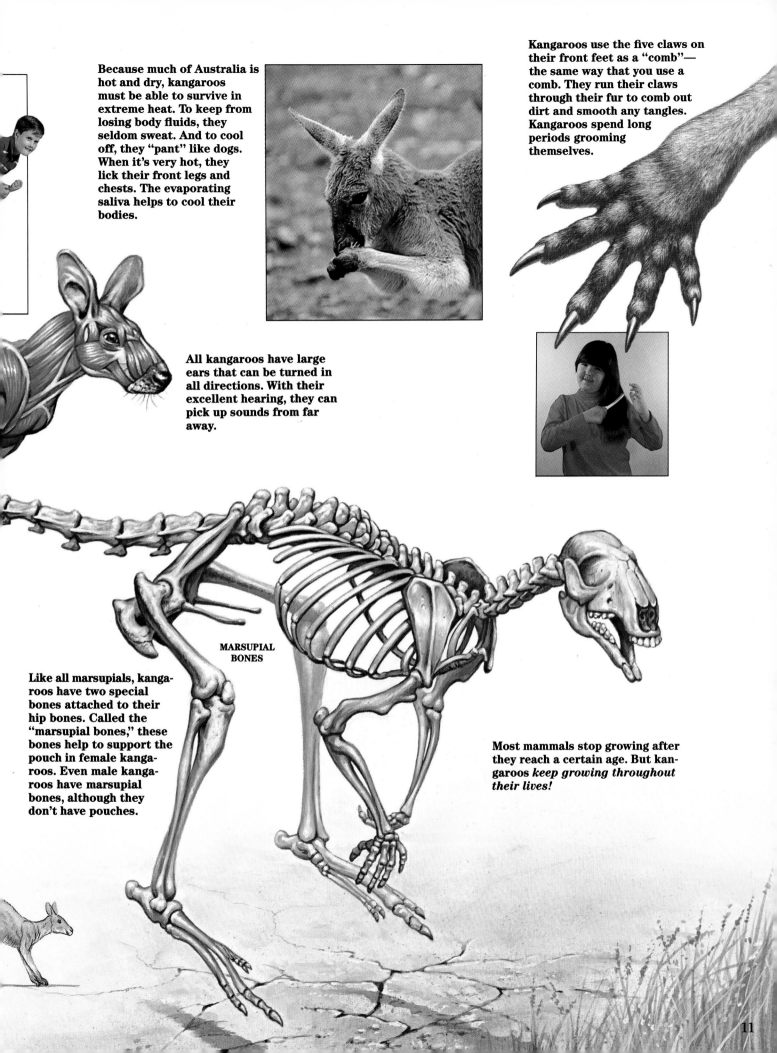

MARSUPIAL BONES

Like all marsupials, kangaroos have two special bones attached to their hip bones. Called the "marsupial bones," these bones help to support the pouch in female kangaroos. Even male kangaroos have marsupial bones, although they don't have pouches.

Most mammals stop growing after they reach a certain age. But kangaroos *keep growing throughout their lives!*

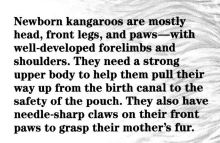

Baby kangaroos, or *joeys,* spend the first five or six months of their lives hidden in their mother's pouch. Warm, safe, and cozy, the pouch is like a cocoon where the baby goes in looking one way and comes out looking completely different!

As you will see below, this tiny newborn makes an amazing journey across its mother's stomach to reach the safety of her pouch. Once inside, the joey doesn't leave—not until six months later, when it emerges as a furry, alert youngster, eager to look around and greet the world.

You've probably seen lots of pictures of a baby kangaroo looking out of its mother's pouch. But what most people don't realize is that this cuddly-looking joey was once a bareskinned baby—blind, deaf, and making its way to its mother's pouch using only instinct and its sense of smell.

◇①

Newborn kangaroos are mostly head, front legs, and paws—with well-developed forelimbs and shoulders. They need a strong upper body to help them pull their way up from the birth canal to the safety of the pouch. They also have needle-sharp claws on their front paws to grasp their mother's fur.

As soon as it is born, the tiny baby begins its steep climb. With no help at all from its mother, the newborn crawls in a snakelike motion through the dense fur. It climbs paw over paw, taking anywhere from three minutes to half an hour to reach the pouch.

Even the biggest kangaroo is *only the size of a bumblebee at birth!* Newborns weigh just 1/28 of an ounce (1 gram) and measure less than 1 inch long (2.5 centimeters). If you were this small when you were born, you would fit into the palm of your mother's hand—with plenty of room to spare!

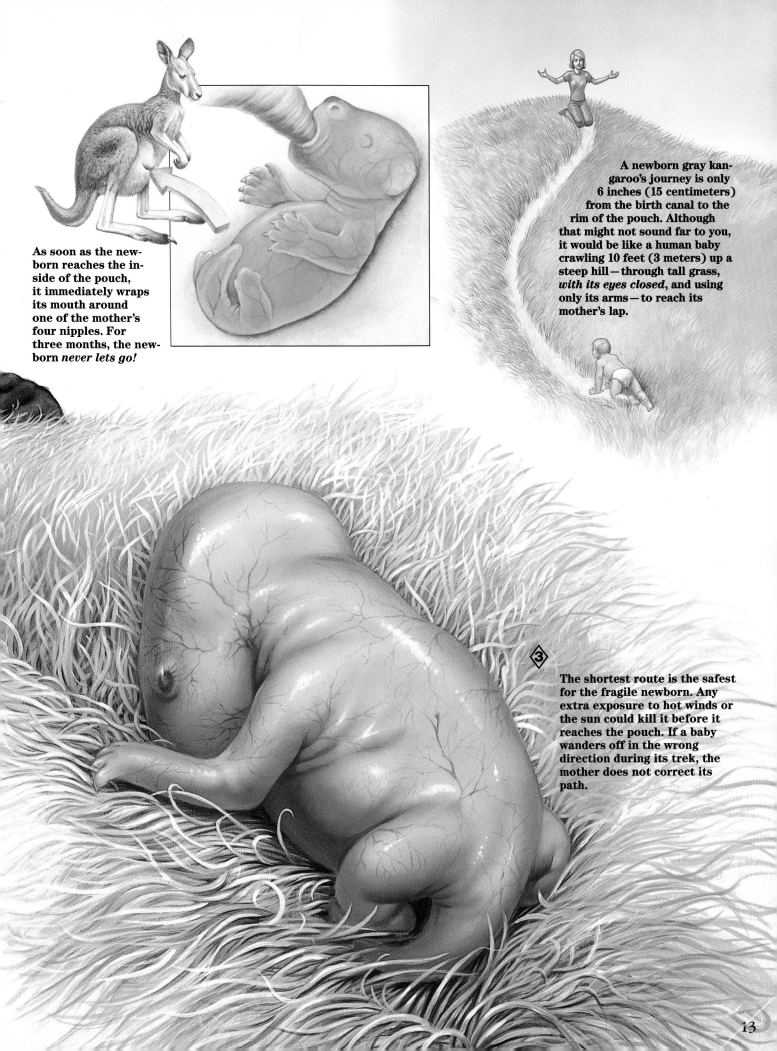

As soon as the newborn reaches the inside of the pouch, it immediately wraps its mouth around one of the mother's four nipples. For three months, the newborn *never lets go!*

A newborn gray kangaroo's journey is only 6 inches (15 centimeters) from the birth canal to the rim of the pouch. Although that might not sound far to you, it would be like a human baby crawling 10 feet (3 meters) up a steep hill — through tall grass, *with its eyes closed*, and using only its arms — to reach its mother's lap.

The shortest route is the safest for the fragile newborn. Any extra exposure to hot winds or the sun could kill it before it reaches the pouch. If a baby wanders off in the wrong direction during its trek, the mother does not correct its path.

Eastern gray kangaroos

Kangaroo mothers and their joeys are very close. By watching their mothers, joeys learn how to graze, groom themselves, and look out for danger. And they copy almost everything she does. Although kangaroos are basically quiet animals, mothers and joeys often communicate by clucking to each other.

At about six or seven months, a joey leaves the pouch for the first time—usually by accident. The youngster may fall out when its mother is cleaning her pouch, or when it leans out of the pouch to graze. At about eight months old, the joey outgrows the pouch for good. But it still pokes its head in from time to time for a drink of milk. And it will stay at its mother's side until it is about one-and-a-half years old and can fend for itself.

Young male kangaroos love to wrestle with their mothers. They push at her with their front paws, and sometimes use their hind-feet to try to knock her off balance. Play fighting helps the joey learn skills he will need when he grows up.

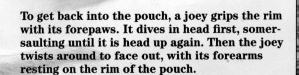

To get back into the pouch, a joey grips the rim with its forepaws. It dives in head first, somer-saulting until it is head up again. Then the joey twists around to face out, with its forearms resting on the rim of the pouch.

Wallaby joeys are favorite targets of wedge-tailed eagles. Often hunting in pairs, one eagle drops down and stuns the victim, knocking it off balance. Then the second eagle swoops down, grabbing the dazed joey with its strong talons and lifting it away.

When chased by wild dogs, or *dingoes*, a mother kangaroo will leap away with her joey in her pouch. Sometimes in mid-flight, she releases the joey into tall grass or bushes. Carrying less weight helps the mother hop faster and escape more easily. It may also save the joey's life—in case she does get caught.

From the pouch, a joey can explore the world safely. It can reach out and sniff objects. And it can pick up grass and try to eat it. Later on, the mother will have to show her joey which grasses to eat. Until it is able to graze on its own, the baby kangaroo's main food is its mother's milk.

17

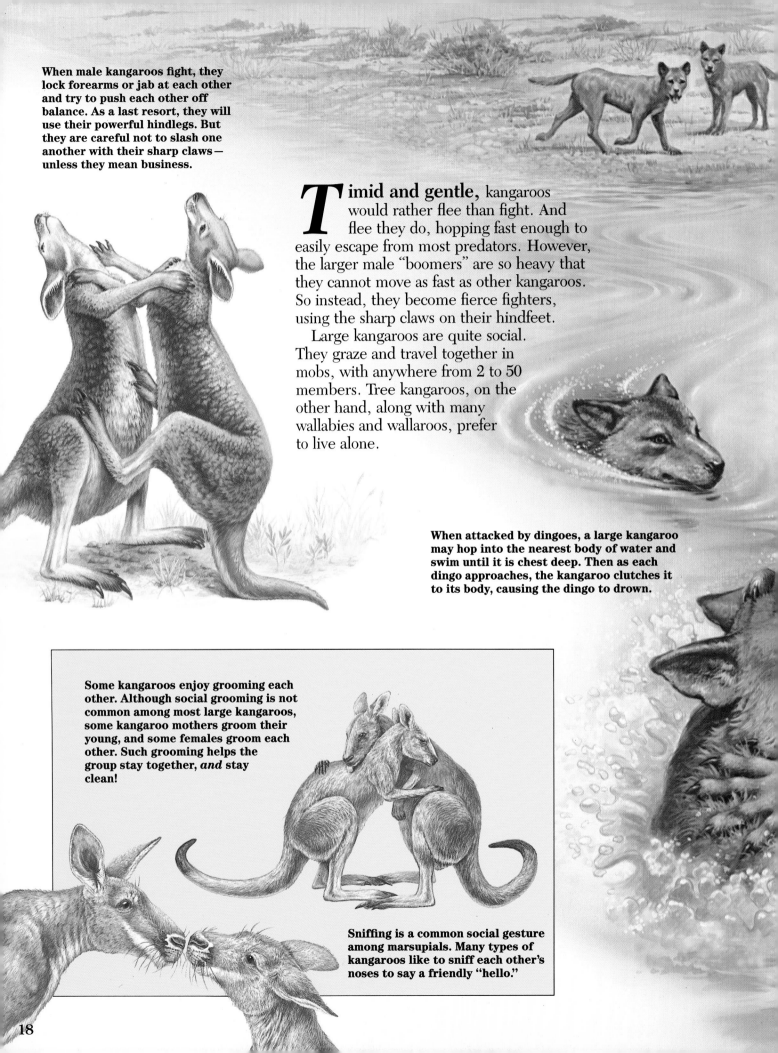

When male kangaroos fight, they lock forearms or jab at each other and try to push each other off balance. As a last resort, they will use their powerful hindlegs. But they are careful not to slash one another with their sharp claws—unless they mean business.

Timid and gentle, kangaroos would rather flee than fight. And flee they do, hopping fast enough to easily escape from most predators. However, the larger male "boomers" are so heavy that they cannot move as fast as other kangaroos. So instead, they become fierce fighters, using the sharp claws on their hindfeet.

Large kangaroos are quite social. They graze and travel together in mobs, with anywhere from 2 to 50 members. Tree kangaroos, on the other hand, along with many wallabies and wallaroos, prefer to live alone.

When attacked by dingoes, a large kangaroo may hop into the nearest body of water and swim until it is chest deep. Then as each dingo approaches, the kangaroo clutches it to its body, causing the dingo to drown.

Some kangaroos enjoy grooming each other. Although social grooming is not common among most large kangaroos, some kangaroo mothers groom their young, and some females groom each other. Such grooming helps the group stay together, *and* stay clean!

Sniffing is a common social gesture among marsupials. Many types of kangaroos like to sniff each other's noses to say a friendly "hello."

When bounding at full speed, large kangaroos can jump *29 feet* (9 meters) or more. One gray kangaroo made *a single jump of 44 feet* (13.5 meters)—longer than a school bus!

Most kangaroos are nighttime feeders, grazing anytime from dusk to dawn. But if it's cloudy and cool, they also may feed during the day. Those kangaroos that graze in the open have become more social—the larger the group, the more eyes there are to watch out for danger.

Besides getting water from plants, kangaroos will drink from streams and water troughs. They will also dig holes to find water if there is no other source! This creates a new water hole, which helps other animals, too.

If the water is shallow, the kangaroo may first catch one dingo and pin it down with its feet. Then it will grab the next one, and push it under the water.

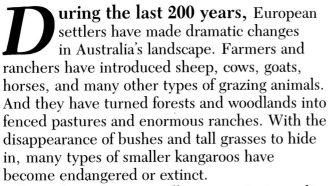

During the last 200 years, European settlers have made dramatic changes in Australia's landscape. Farmers and ranchers have introduced sheep, cows, goats, horses, and many other types of grazing animals. And they have turned forests and woodlands into fenced pastures and enormous ranches. With the disappearance of bushes and tall grasses to hide in, many types of smaller kangaroos have become endangered or extinct.

Large kangaroos are still common in Australia, but there is concern that hunting—as well as drought and human changes to the land—will eventually threaten the kangaroo population. Australians are struggling to find ways to make room for both the kangaroos and the ranchers' livestock.

About two million years ago, a giant kangaroo called *Procoptodon goliah* (pro-COP-tuh-don go-LIE-uh) lived in Australia. It weighed 500 pounds and may have stood 9 feet tall. The average modern kangaroo stands about 6 feet tall and weighs only 160 pounds. The giant kangaroo disappeared about 40,000 years ago—probably driven to extinction by changes in its habitat.

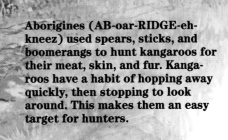

Aborigines (AB-oar-RIDGE-eh-kneez) used spears, sticks, and boomerangs to hunt kangaroos for their meat, skin, and fur. Kangaroos have a habit of hopping away quickly, then stopping to look around. This makes them an easy target for hunters.

An ancient aboriginal legend told of a huge windstorm blowing large, strange-looking creatures through the air. The animals tried so hard to touch the ground that their back legs grew very long. When they finally fell, they quickly hopped away. And that, according to the story, is how kangaroos came to Australia!

In the early 1900s, kangaroos were pitted against men in boxing matches. Because kangaroos are natural fighters, they needed no training to learn how to hit. But their human opponents had to be careful to avoid the kangaroos' dangerous claws— one swift kick from a big kangaroo could kill anyone.

Sheep ranching actually helps some kangaroos by providing them with additional sources of water. But some ranchers put too many sheep on a piece of land, and they overgraze. This wipes out *all* plant life—and the land becomes useless for both livestock and kangaroos.

Leap into these kangaroo activities. Use what you have learned about kangaroos to complete these two pages of fun things to do.

Jumping for Joey

Gray kangaroos have been known to jump 44 feet (13.5 meters) in one leap. Imagine that you are a kangaroo. How far can you jump in one leap? First, try the standing broad jump. Begin by standing still with your feet together. Then take a big leap forward. Measure how far you jumped. Next, try the running broad jump. Begin by running. Then take a big leap forward. Which way could you jump the farthest?

Like a kangaroo, you could probably jump farther once you were already moving. But a kangaroo not only can jump farther once it is moving, it also uses less energy. It is the only animal that uses less energy the faster it goes!

1.

2.

3.

4.

5.

6.

7.

Kangaroos are among the favorite subjects of aboriginal artists in Australia. Using natural materials to make their paints, the aborigines create beautiful bark paintings like the ones shown below and at right. Notice the bold outlines of the kangaroos and Australian plants. Some of the kangaroos are intricately textured with dots and lines.

Kangaroo Secret Code

The letters in the grids below form a secret code. Each letter in the alphabet is represented by a special symbol. For example, A= ⌐ ; N=□ ; X=▣ . Use the secret code to discover each of the eight mystery words below. Write the letter that goes with each symbol.

A	B	C
D	E	F
G	H	I

J	K	L
M	N	O
P	Q	R

S	T	U
V	W	X
Y	Z

A Mob Scene

There are 18 kangaroos hiding in this mob scene. How many of them can you find?

8. ⌐ ⌐⌐ ⌐⌐ ⌐ ⌐ ⌐ ⌐ ⌐

1. Mob 2. Joey 3. Pouch 4. Wallaby 5. Kangaroo 6. Wallaroo 7. Marsupial 8. Australia

Kangaroo Bark Art

Follow these instructions to make an artwork in the style of the aboriginal bark paintings. You will need: *a brown paper bag, a spoon or popsicle stick, and crayons.*

1. Tear an 8 × 8 inch (20 × 20 cm) square out of a paper bag. Color one side of the square with a thick layer of yellow crayon. Press firmly. Then color over the yellow crayon with a layer of orange crayon.

2. Use a dark brown crayon to color over the orange crayon. Press lightly, but cover the entire space with brown crayon.

3. On scratch paper, design a kangaroo using simple lines, like those used in the aboriginal bark paintings. Then carefully etch your design in the crayon layers. Use the spoon or popsicle stick to etch lines, textures, and solid areas.

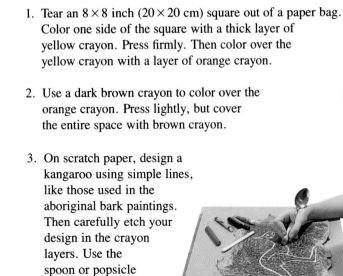

Index